Kids' Felt Cuties

GO FISHING FOR FUN WITH SOFT TOYS

From a magnetic game to piggy banks for flexible spending, the fun designs in this colorful collection will keep kids entertained. Patterns and step-by-step instructions make them all easy to craft. Don't be surprised if the kids want to help!

LEISURE ARTS, INC. • Maumelle, Arkansas

SIMPLE FLOWER CROWN

Finished Size: 22" x 5"

SHOPPING LIST

- ☐ 23" x 12" piece of light pink felt
- ☐ 1 sheet of pink felt
- ☐ 1 sheet of light yellow felt
- ☐ 1 sheet of green felt
- ☐ 1 sheet of light green felt
- ☐ light pink 6-strand embroidery floss
- ☐ embroidery needle
- ☐ 3"-4" of 1/2" wide elastic
- ☐ low-temp glue gun and glue sticks
- ☐ tracing paper

*Please read **General Instructions**, pages 30-31, before beginning project. Follow **Using Patterns**, page 30, to adjust pattern size.*

CUTTING

***Note:** Use patterns on page 22.*

1. Cut 2 crowns from light pink felt.
2. Cut 12 large flower petals and 18 small flower petals from pink felt.
3. Cut 1 strip 1 1/4" x 4 1/2" and 2 strips 1" x 3" from light yellow felt.
4. Cut 1 large leaf and 5 medium leaves from green felt.
5. Cut 1 large leaf, 3 medium leaves, and 3 small leaves from light green felt.

TO MAKE THE CROWN

***Note:** Refer to **Embroidery Stitches**, page 31, for stitch techniques. Use 3 strands of floss for all stitching.*

1. Stack the crown pieces and secure them with glue. Do not glue near the edges; you will be stitching there later.
2. To make a large flower center, fold the large strip of light yellow felt in half lengthwise and glue the edge **(Fig. 1)**. Make cuts in the folded edge about 1/4" deep and 1/8" apart **(Fig. 2)**. Place a small drop of glue on 1 end and roll the rectangle tightly in the center. Keep rolling and adding a drop of glue ever so often until you reach the end **(Fig. 3)**.

3. To make the large flower, place 1 small drop of glue near the bottom of 1 large petal and glue it to the flower center. Repeat with 3 large petals around the center. Glue the remaining large petals in layers around the center until you are pleased with the flower; you may not use all the petals. Allow the glue to cool for at least 5 minutes. Trim the bottom flat so it can be glued to the crown. Use a generous amount of glue and glue the flower to the center of the crown.

4. Glue 1 large and 3 medium green leaves and 1 large, 1 medium, and 2 small light green leaves around the flower.

5. Repeat Steps 2-3 to make 2 small flowers using the small strips for the centers and the small petals. You will need 8-9 petals per flower.

6. Glue 1 small flower on each side of the large flower. Glue remaining leaves around the flowers.

7. Using a Running Stitch, stitch all around the crown edges using embroidery floss. When you reach the back edges of the crown, insert the elastic piece between the layers, adjusting it to fit head and securing it on each end as you stitch.

8. Finish by trimming all along the edges of the crown.

Fig. 1

Fig. 2

Fig. 3

Jeweled Crown instructions on page 7.

FLORAL HEADBAND

Finished Size: 14"

SHOPPING LIST

- ☐ 3" x 14" piece of cream felt
- ☐ 2 sheets of plum felt
- ☐ 1 sheet of light pink felt
- ☐ 1 sheet of light yellow felt
- ☐ 1 sheet of gold felt
- ☐ 1 sheet of gray felt
- ☐ 1 sheet of green felt
- ☐ 1 sheet of light green felt
- ☐ 28" of 5/8" wide cream ribbon
- ☐ 14" of natural hemp-wrapped wire
- ☐ low-temp glue gun and glue sticks

Please read ***General Instructions****, pages 30-31, before beginning project. Follow* ***Using Patterns****, page 30, to adjust pattern size.*

CUTTING

Note: *Use patterns on page 22.*

1. Cut 2 strips 1" x 14" from cream felt.
2. Cut 50 large flower petals from plum felt.
3. Cut 30 large flower petals from light pink felt.
4. Cut 2 strips 2" x 7" from light yellow felt for large mums.
5. Cut 2 strips 1 1/2" x 6 1/2" from gold felt for small mums.
6. Cut 8 strips 3/4" x 4" from gray felt for flower centers.
7. Cut desired large, medium, and small leaves from green and light green felt. We used 4-5 leaves on each side.

TO MAKE THE HEADBAND

1. Stack the cream felt strips and secure them with glue along the long edges. Do not glue the short edges closed; you will be inserting ribbon there later.

2. Glue the wire to the center on one side of the cream felt strips. To make the headband, bend the wire to fit the head.

3. To make a flower center, make cuts in one edge of a gray felt strip about 1/2" deep and 1/8" apart **(Fig. 1)**. Place a small drop of glue on 1 end and roll the rectangle tightly in the center. Keep rolling and adding a drop of glue ever so often until you reach the end **(Fig. 2)**. Make a total of 8 flower centers.

4. To make the large light pink flower, place 1 small drop of glue near the bottom of 1 large petal and glue it to the flower center. Repeat with 3 large petals around the center. Glue up to 6 large petals in layers around the center until you are pleased with the flower; you may not use all the petals. Allow the glue to cool for at least 5 minutes.

5. Repeat Step 4 to make a total of 3 light pink large flowers and 5 plum large flowers.

6. To make a large mum, fold the strip of light yellow felt in half lengthwise and glue the edge **(Fig. 3)**. Make cuts in the folded edge about 3/4" deep and 1/4" apart **(Fig. 4)**. Place a small drop of glue on 1 end and roll the rectangle tightly in the center. Keep rolling and adding a drop of glue ever so often until you reach the end **(Fig. 5)**.

7. Repeat Step 6 to make a total of 2 light yellow large mums. Repeat to make 2 gold small mums, making cuts in the folded edge about 1/2" deep and 1/4" apart.

8. Glue flowers and mums to the headband as desired with generous amounts of glue. Glue the leaves near the ends of the headband as desired.

9. Glue one ribbon end between the felt layers on each end of the headband.

10. Trim the felt on the headband to desired width behind the flowers, leaving the headband wider at the ends.

Fig. 1

Fig. 2

Fig. 3

Fig. 4

Fig. 5

STAR WAND

SHOPPING LIST

- ☐ 1 sheet of yellow felt
- ☐ yellow 6-strand embroidery floss
- ☐ embroidery needle
- ☐ gold glitter glue
- ☐ 18" of 5/16" diameter wooden dowel
- ☐ 8 assorted narrow ribbons 6"-13" long
- ☐ polyester fiberfill
- ☐ low-temp glue gun and glue sticks

*Please read **General Instructions**, pages 30-31, before beginning project. Follow **Using Patterns**, page 30, to adjust pattern size.*

TO MAKE THE STAR WAND

***Note:** Use pattern on page 22. Refer to **Embroidery Stitches**, page 31, for stitch techniques. Use 3 strands of floss for all stitching.*

1. Cut 2 stars from yellow felt. Stack the stars on top of each other.
2. Using a Running Stitch, stitch around the star, starting and ending near the bottom and leaving an opening at the bottom. Stuff the star with fiberfill.
3. Glue the ribbons about 2 1/2" from 1 end of the dowel.
4. Place glue on the end of the dowel with the ribbons and quickly insert the dowel into the opening in the star until the ribbon ends are covered. Allow the glue to cool for a few minutes.
5. Finish stitching a Running Stitch around the bottom of the star to close the opening.
6. Add glitter glue drops on one side of the star as desired; allow to dry.

Floral Headband instructions on page 4.

JEWELED CROWN

Finished Size: 22" x 5"

SHOPPING LIST

- ☐ 23" x 12" piece of blue felt
- ☐ 1 sheet of gold felt
- ☐ gold 6-strand embroidery floss
- ☐ embroidery needle
- ☐ nine 7/8" diameter jewel stones
- ☐ 3"-4" of 1/2" wide elastic
- ☐ low-temp glue gun and glue sticks

*Please read **General Instructions**, pages 30-31, before beginning project. Follow **Using Patterns**, page 30, to adjust pattern size.*

CUTTING

***Note:** Use pattern on page 22.*

1. Cut 2 crowns from blue felt.
2. Cut 2 strips 1 3/8" wide and the length of the sheet from gold felt. Butt the ends together and use gold embroidery floss to whipstitch ends together to make 1 long strip. Trim strip to 22" long.

TO MAKE THE CROWN

***Note:** Refer to **Embroidery Stitches**, page 31, for stitch techniques. Use 3 strands of floss for all stitching.*

1. Stack the crown pieces and secure them with glue. Do not glue near the edges; you will be stitching there later.
2. Glue the strip around the crown about 1/4" from the bottom edge; again, do not glue near the edges. Trim ends as needed.
3. Using a Running Stitch, stitch along all edges of the gold strip and around all edges of the crown. When you reach the back edges of the crown, insert the elastic piece between the layers, adjusting it to fit head and securing it on each end as you stitch.
4. Glue the jewels along the gold strip, spacing as desired.
5. Finish by trimming all along the edges of the crown.

Bella's
Garden

GARDEN CRATE

Finished Size: 10" x 13" x 6"

SHOPPING LIST

- ☐ 10" x 13" x 6" wood crate
- ☐ $^{1}/_{2}$ yard of 72" wide brown felt
- ☐ 1 sheet of black felt
- ☐ brown 6-strand embroidery floss
- ☐ embroidery needle
- ☐ $2^{3}/_{8}$" x 2" piece of white paper
- ☐ polyester fiberfill
- ☐ low-temp glue gun and glue sticks

Please read ***General Instructions****, pages 30-31, before beginning project.*

CUTTING

1. Cut 4 dirt rows 14" x 16" from brown felt.
2. Cut 2 garden signs $3^{1}/_{4}$" x 4" from black felt.

TO MAKE THE GARDEN CRATE

Note: *Refer to* ***Embroidery Stitches****, page 31, for stitch techniques. Use 3 strands of floss for all stitching.*

1. To make 1 dirt row, overlap the short edges on 1 dirt row piece about $^{1}/_{2}$" and glue in place; allow the glue to cool. Using a loose Running Stitch and leaving long ends at beginning and end, stitch around each open edge using brown embroidery floss.
2. Pull the floss tails tight to close 1 end; tie a knot. Stuff the tube with fiberfill and pull the remaining floss ends tight to close the remaining end. Repeat to make 4 dirt pieces.
3. Stuff the dirt rows into the crate.
4. Glue the black garden signs together. Personalize your garden on the white paper piece. Glue the paper to the sign. Glue the sign to the crate.

FLOWERS

Finished Size: $4^{3}/_{8}$" x $8^{1}/_{4}$"

SHOPPING LIST

Note: *Supplies listed are for making 3 flowers.*

- ☐ 2 sheets of green felt
- ☐ 1 sheet of pink felt
- ☐ 1 sheet of hot pink felt
- ☐ 1 sheet of purple felt
- ☐ 1 sheet of yellow felt
- ☐ yellow, pink, hot pink, and purple 6-strand embroidery floss
- ☐ embroidery needle
- ☐ 3 jumbo wood craft sticks
- ☐ low-temp glue gun and glue sticks

Please read ***General Instructions****, pages 30-31, before beginning project. Follow* ***Using Patterns****, page 30, to adjust pattern size.*

CUTTING

Note: *Use patterns on page 23.*

1. Cut 6 leaves and 3 stems $2^{1}/_{2}$" x 6" from green felt.
2. Cut 2 flowers **each** from pink, hot pink, and purple felt.
3. Cut 3 flower centers from yellow felt.

TO MAKE THE FLOWERS

Note: *Refer to* ***Embroidery Stitches****, page 31, for stitch techniques. Use 3 strands of floss for all stitching.*

1. Using a Running Stitch, stitch 1 flower center to 1 flower using yellow embroidery floss.
2. Using a Running Stitch and leaving an opening for the stem, stitch 2 flowers (1 with a center, 1 without a center) together using embroidery floss matching the flower.
3. Glue 1 stem around 1 craft stick. Glue the stem into the opening in the flower. Glue 2 leaves to the stem.
4. Finish stitching the front flower at the opening. These stitches will be decorative and only through 1 layer of felt.
5. Repeat Steps 1-4 to make a total of 3 flowers.

CABBAGES

Finished Size: 5" diameter

SHOPPING LIST

Note: *Supplies listed are for making 2 cabbages.*

- ☐ 4 sheets of light green felt
- ☐ light green 6-strand embroidery floss
- ☐ embroidery needle
- ☐ polyester fiberfill
- ☐ low-temp glue gun and glue sticks
- ☐ tracing paper

*Please read **General Instructions**, pages 30-31, before beginning project. Follow **Using Patterns**, page 30, to use patterns.*

CUTTING

Note: *Use patterns on page 24.*

1. Cut 2 cabbage centers, 2 outer cabbage leaf pieces, and 2 inner cabbage leaf pieces from light green felt.

TO MAKE THE CABBAGES

Note: *Refer to **Embroidery Stitches**, page 31, for stitch techniques. Use 4 strands of floss for all stitching.*

1. Leaving long ends, stitch loose Running Stitches around the edge of 1 cabbage center. Pull the floss tight to create a round cabbage center; stuff with fiberfill. When full, pull the floss ends tight and knot.
2. Use glue to attach the inner cabbage leaves to the center. Gluing as you go, wrap the leaves around the center, pinching small tucks in the bottom of some of the leaves to create a fuller look.
3. Repeat Step 2 to attach the outer cabbage leaves.
4. If desired, trim some of the leaf edges unevenly to look more realistic.
5. Repeat Steps 1-4 to make a total of 2 cabbages.

CARROTS

Finished Size: 2 1/2" x 8 1/2"

SHOPPING LIST

Note: *Supplies listed are for making 4 carrots.*

- ☐ 2 sheets of orange felt
- ☐ 1 sheet of green felt
- ☐ 1 sheet of light green felt
- ☐ orange 6-strand embroidery floss
- ☐ embroidery needle
- ☐ polyester fiberfill
- ☐ low-temp glue gun and glue sticks

*Please read **General Instructions**, pages 30-31, before beginning project. Follow **Using Patterns**, page 30, to adjust pattern size.*

CUTTING

Note: *Use patterns on page 23.*

1. Cut 8 carrots from orange felt.
2. Cut 4 large carrot tops from green felt.
3. Cut 4 small carrot tops from light green felt.

TO MAKE THE CARROTS

Note: *Refer to **Embroidery Stitches**, page 31, for stitch techniques. Use 4 strands of floss for all stitching unless otherwise indicated.*

1. Using a Backstitch, stitch the carrot details on 4 carrots using orange embroidery floss.
2. Using a Running Stitch and leaving the top open, stitch 2 carrots (1 stitched, 1 unstitched) together using orange embroidery floss.
3. Stuff the carrot with fiberfill. Insert 1 large carrot top and 1 small carrot top in the top opening. Stitch the opening closed using a Running Stitch and 3 strands of orange floss and securing the carrot tops in the stitching as you go. Add a drop of glue between the tops to hold them together.
4. Repeat Steps 2-3 to make a total of 4 carrots.

RADISHES

Finished Size: 4 1/2" x 5 1/2"

SHOPPING LIST

Note: *Supplies listed are for making 3 radishes.*

- ☐ 1 sheet of magenta felt
- ☐ 2 sheets of green felt
- ☐ magenta and green 6-strand embroidery floss
- ☐ embroidery needle
- ☐ polyester fiberfill

*Please read **General Instructions**, pages 30-31, before beginning project. Follow **Using Patterns**, page 30, to adjust pattern size.*

CUTTING

Note: *Use patterns on page 23.*

1. Cut 6 radishes from magenta felt.
2. Cut 6 leaves from green felt.

TO MAKE THE RADISHES

Note: *Refer to **Embroidery Stitches**, page 31, for stitch techniques. Use 6 strands of floss for all stitching.*

1. Using a Running Stitch and leaving the top open, stitch 2 radishes together using magenta embroidery floss.

2. Place 2 leaves together. Using green embroidery floss, add a large stitch through both layers in the center of each leaf and pull it tight to create a pucker; bring thread between layers and knot.

3. Stuff the radish with fiberfill. Insert leaf in the top opening. Stitch the opening closed using a Running Stitch and magenta floss and securing the leaf in the stitching as you go.

4. Repeat Steps 1-3 to make a total of 2 radishes.

PIGGY COIN BANK

Finished Size: 5" x 4"

SHOPPING LIST

Note: *Supplies listed are for making 1 bank.*

- ☐ 1 sheet of pink, blue, or gray felt
- ☐ 6-strand embroidery floss to match felt
- ☐ embroidery needle

Please read ***General Instructions****, pages 30-31, before beginning project. Follow* ***Using Patterns****, page 30.*

CUTTING

Note: *Use patterns on page 24.*

1. Cut 2 pig bodies from felt.
2. Cut 1 tail from felt.

TO MAKE THE BANK

Note: *Refer to* ***Embroidery Stitches****, page 31, for stitch techniques. Use 2 strands of floss for all stitching.*

1. Using a Backstitch, stitch around the coin opening.

2. Stack 2 pig bodies together. Using a Backstitch, stitch around the body, catching the tail between the layers in the stitching as you go.

DEER MASK

Finished Size: $9^{3}/_{4}$" x $6^{3}/_{4}$"

SHOPPING LIST

- ☐ 2 sheets of brown felt
- ☐ 1 sheet of tan felt
- ☐ 1 sheet of black felt
- ☐ 1 sheet of pink felt
- ☐ brown, tan, and black 6-strand embroidery floss
- ☐ embroidery needle
- ☐ 10" of 3/4" wide elastic
- ☐ low-temp glue gun and glue sticks

*Please read **General Instructions**, pages 30-31, before beginning project. Follow **Using Patterns**, page 30, to adjust pattern size.*

CUTTING

***Note:** Use patterns on pages 25-26.*

1. Cut 2 base masks (using eye placement for deer), 2 outer ears, and 3 spots from brown felt.
2. Cut 1 forehead from tan felt.
3. Cut 2 inner ears from pink felt.
4. Cut 1 nose from black felt.

TO MAKE THE MASK

Note: *Refer to* ***Embroidery Stitches****, page 31, for stitch techniques. Use 3 strands of floss for all stitching unless otherwise indicated.*

1. Place the forehead on 1 base mask and secure it with glue. Do not glue near the edges; you will be stitching there later. Using a Running Stitch, stitch around the forehead using tan embroidery floss.

2. Using a Backstitch and Straight Stitches and 6 strands of floss, stitch the eyelashes on the mask using black floss.

3. Stack the mask on top of the remaining base mask and secure it with glue. Do not glue near the edges. Using a Running Stitch, stitch around the eyes using brown embroidery floss.

4. Place a drop of glue at the bottom edge of the inner ear; pinch the ear together and hold until the glue cools. Glue the inner ear to an outer ear. Repeat for the remaining inner and outer ears. Glue the ears between the two base masks with small drops of glue.

5. Insert 1 end of the elastic between the mask layers below the ears; pin. Using a Running Stitch and beginning at the edge of the forehead, stitch the mask layers together, securing the elastic end in the stitching as you go. When you reach the other side, insert the opposite end of the elastic between the layers, adjusting the elastic to fit head, and continue stitching to secure elastic end. Continue stitching around mask, ending stitching at the forehead.

6. Using a Running Stitch, stitch around the nose using black floss. Glue the nose to the mask. Glue the spots to the forehead.

7. Make sure the mask layers are glued together securely. If necessary, trim the eye opening layers even.

FOX MASK

Finished Size: $9\frac{1}{4}$" x $6\frac{1}{2}$"

SHOPPING LIST

- ☐ 2 sheets of orange felt
- ☐ 1 sheet of white felt
- ☐ 1 sheet of black felt
- ☐ orange and black 6-strand embroidery floss
- ☐ embroidery needle
- ☐ 10" of $\frac{3}{4}$" wide elastic
- ☐ low-temp glue gun and glue sticks

Please read ***General Instructions****, pages 30-31, before beginning project. Follow* ***Using Patterns****, page 30, to adjust pattern size.*

CUTTING

Note: *Use patterns on pages 25-26.*

1. Cut 1 base mask (using eye placement for fox), 1 fox mask, and 2 outer ears from orange felt.
2. Cut 2 inner ears and 2 whiskers from white felt.
3. Cut 1 nose from black felt.

TO MAKE THE MASK

Note: *Refer to* ***Embroidery Stitches****, page 31, for stitch techniques. Use 3 strands of floss for all stitching.*

1. Stack the fox mask on top of the base mask and secure them with glue. Do not glue near the edges; you will be stitching there later. Using a Running Stitch, stitch around the eyes using orange embroidery floss.

2. Glue each inner ear to an outer ear. Glue the ears between the base mask and the fox mask with small drops of glue.

3. Glue the whiskers and nose to the fox mask. Using a Running Stitch, stitch around the nose using black embroidery floss.

4. Insert 1 end of the elastic between the mask layers below 1 ear. Using a Running Stitch and securing the elastic end in the stitching as you go, stitch the mask layers together across the top of the head. When you reach the other side, insert the opposite end of the elastic between the layers, adjusting the elastic to fit head, and continue stitching to secure elastic end. End stitching below the opposite ear.

5. Make sure the mask layers are glued together securely. If necessary, trim the eye opening layers even.

RACOON MASK

Finished Size: $9^{1}/_{2}$" x $7^{1}/_{2}$"

SHOPPING LIST

- ☐ 2 sheets of gray felt
- ☐ 1 sheet of black felt
- ☐ black and gray 6-strand embroidery floss
- ☐ embroidery needle
- ☐ 10" of $^{3}/_{4}$" wide elastic
- ☐ low-temp glue gun and glue sticks

Please read ***General Instructions****, pages 30-31, before beginning project. Follow* ***Using Patterns****, page 30, to adjust pattern size.*

CUTTING

Note: *Use patterns on page 25.*

1. Cut 2 base masks (using eye placement for racoon) and 2 ears from gray felt.
2. Cut 1 nose and 2 eye bands from black felt.

TO MAKE THE MASK

Note: *Refer to* ***Embroidery Stitches****, page 31, for stitch techniques. Use 3 strands of floss for all stitching unless otherwise indicated.*

1. Stack the base masks together and secure them with glue. Do not glue near the edges; you will be stitching there later.

2. Glue the eye bands and nose to the base mask leaving the outer edges loose. Glue the ears between the two base masks with small drops of glue. Using a Running Stitch, stitch around the eyes and nose using black embroidery floss.

3. Insert 1 end of the elastic between the mask layers behind the eye band. Using a Running Stitch and securing the elastic end in the stitching as you go, stitch the mask layers together. When you reach the other side, insert the opposite end of the elastic between the layers, adjusting the elastic to fit head, and continue stitching to secure elastic end. Stitch around the mask to where you began.

4. Make sure the mask layers are glued together securely. If necessary, trim the eye opening layers even.

FISHING GAME

Finished Size: 32" diameter

SHOPPING LIST

- ☐ 32" diameter circle of blue felt
- ☐ 1 sheet of gray felt
- ☐ 18" of 5/16" wood dowel
- ☐ 40" of white rope
- ☐ red and grey 6-strand embroidery floss
- ☐ heavy-duty magnet
- ☐ low-temp glue gun and glue sticks

Please read ***General Instructions****, pages 30-31, before beginning project.*

TO MAKE THE FISHING POLE

1. Attach the white rope to the dowel in three spots. Add a drop of glue near the handle and the middle of the pole. Allowing a little slack between spots, hold the rope at the handle and the middle until the glue is cool. Add a drop of glue near the tip of the pole; wrap the rope around the tip 2-3 times.

2. Use red embroidery floss to wrap the handle of the pole for about 2³/₄"; glue to secure. Repeat to wrap and secure the middle for about 1/4" and the tip for about 1/2".

3. Glue the magnet to the end of the rope. Fold a piece of gray felt over the magnet; trim slightly larger than the magnet. Whipstitch the edges together around the edges of the magnet. Add glue if necessary. Use gray embroidery floss to wrap the rope just above the magnet for about 1/2"; glue to secure.

PARROT FISH

Finished Size: 6 1/2" x 3"

SHOPPING LIST

Note: *Supplies listed are for making 1 fish.*

- ☐ 1 sheet of red felt
- ☐ 1 sheet of yellow felt
- ☐ 1 sheet of turquoise felt
- ☐ 1 sheet of white felt
- ☐ 1 sheet of black felt
- ☐ red 6-strand embroidery floss
- ☐ embroidery needle
- ☐ heavy-duty magnet
- ☐ polyester fiberfill
- ☐ low-temp glue gun and glue sticks

Please read ***General Instructions****, pages 30-31, before beginning project. Follow* ***Using Patterns****, page 30, to adjust pattern size.*

CUTTING

Note: *Use patterns on page 28.*

1. Cut 2 bodies from red felt.
2. Cut 2 stripes from yellow felt.
3. Cut 2 stripes and 2 tail fins from turquoise felt.
4. Cut 2 outer eyes from white felt.
5. Cut 2 inner eyes from black felt.

TO MAKE THE PARROT FISH

Note: *Refer to* ***Embroidery Stitches****, page 31, for stitch techniques. Use 3 strands of floss for all stitching unless otherwise indicated.*

1. Glue the magnet near the front on one body; be sure to leave enough space to stitch the fish together later.

2. Place 1 tail fin on 1 body. Using a Backstitch, stitch the detail lines on the tail fin through the body using 2 strands of red embroidery floss. Repeat for remaining body and tail fin.

3. Stack the bodies. Using a Running Stitch, stitch the bodies together, leaving an opening at the bottom for stuffing and using red embroidery floss.

4. Stuff fish with fiberfill. Continue the Running Stitch to close the opening.

5. Glue the eyes and stripes to each side of the fish.

GLOW FISH

Finished Size: 6 3/4" x 2 1/4"

SHOPPING LIST

Note: *Supplies listed are for making 3 fish.*

- ☐ 2 sheets of neon green felt
- ☐ 1 sheet of orange felt
- ☐ 1 sheet of white felt
- ☐ 1 sheet of black felt
- ☐ neon green 6-strand embroidery floss
- ☐ embroidery needle
- ☐ 3 heavy-duty magnets
- ☐ polyester fiberfill
- ☐ low-temp glue gun and glue sticks

*Please read **General Instructions**, pages 30-31, before beginning project. Follow **Using Patterns**, page 30, to adjust pattern size.*

CUTTING

Note: *Use patterns on page 28.*

1. Cut 6 bodies from neon green felt.
2. Cut 3 fins from orange felt.
3. Cut 6 outer eyes from white felt.
4. Cut 6 inner eyes from black felt.

TO MAKE THE GLOW FISH

Note: *Refer to **Embroidery Stitches**, page 31, for stitch techniques. Use 2 strands of floss for all stitching.*

1. Glue a magnet near the front on one body; be sure to leave enough space to stitch the fish together later.
2. Glue the fin to the back of one body. Be careful not to put glue in the area where you will stitch to assemble the fish.
3. Stack two bodies together. Using a Running Stitch, stitch the bodies together, leaving an opening at the bottom for stuffing.
4. Stuff fish with fiberfill. Continue the Running Stitch to close the opening.
5. Glue the eyes to each side of the fish.
6. Repeat Steps 1-5 to make a total of 3 Glow Fish.

PINKY FISH

Finished Size: 5" x 2"

SHOPPING LIST

Note: *Supplies listed are for making 1 fish.*

- ☐ 1 sheet of pink felt
- ☐ 1 sheet of white felt
- ☐ 1 sheet of black felt
- ☐ neon green and pink 6-strand embroidery floss
- ☐ embroidery needle
- ☐ heavy-duty magnet
- ☐ polyester fiberfill
- ☐ low-temp glue gun and glue sticks

*Please read **General Instructions**, pages 30-31, before beginning project. Follow **Using Patterns**, page 30, to adjust pattern size.*

CUTTING

Note: *Use patterns on page 27.*

1. Cut 2 bodies from pink felt.
2. Cut 2 outer eyes from white felt.
3. Cut 2 inner eyes from black felt.

TO MAKE THE PINKY FISH

Note: *Refer to **Embroidery Stitches**, page 31, for stitch techniques. Use 2 strands of floss for all stitching unless otherwise indicated.*

1. Using a Backstitch and 4 strands of neon green embroidery floss, stitch detail lines on each fish body.
2. Glue the magnet near the front on one body; be sure to leave enough space to stitch the fish together later.
3. Stack the bodies. Using a Running Stitch, stitch the bodies together, leaving an opening at the bottom for stuffing.
4. Stuff fish with fiberfill. Continue the Running Stitch to close the opening.
5. Glue the eyes to each side of the fish.

BLUE RUNNER FISH

Finished Size: 6 1/2" x 2 3/4"

SHOPPING LIST

***Note:** Supplies listed are for making 2 fish.*

- ☐ 1 sheet of teal felt
- ☐ 1 sheet of gold felt
- ☐ 1 sheet of white felt
- ☐ 1 sheet of black felt
- ☐ gold and teal 6-strand embroidery floss
- ☐ embroidery needle
- ☐ 2 heavy-duty magnets
- ☐ polyester fiberfill
- ☐ low-temp glue gun and glue sticks

*Please read **General Instructions**, pages 30-31, before beginning project. Follow **Using Patterns**, page 30, to adjust pattern size.*

CUTTING

***Note:** Use patterns on page 28.*

1. Cut 4 bodies from teal felt.
2. Cut 2 top fins and 2 tail fins from gold felt.
3. Cut 4 outer eyes from white felt.
4. Cut 4 inner eyes from black felt.

TO MAKE THE BLUE RUNNER FISH

***Note:** Refer to **Embroidery Stitches**, page 31, for stitch techniques. Use 3 strands of floss for all stitching unless otherwise indicated.*

1. Using a Backstitch, stitch the detail lines on 1 tail fin using 2 strands of gold embroidery floss. Repeat for another tail fin. Glue tail fins together.

2. Using a Backstitch, stitch the gills on 1 body using 2 strands of gold embroidery floss. Repeat for another body.

3. Glue a magnet near the front on one body; be sure to leave enough space to stitch the fish together later.

4. Glue the top fin and tail fin to the back of one body. Be careful not to put glue in the area where you will stitch to assemble the fish.

5. Stack the bodies. Using a Running Stitch, stitch the bodies together, leaving an opening at the bottom for stuffing using teal embroidery floss.

6. Stuff fish with fiberfill. Continue the Running Stitch to close the opening.

7. Glue the eyes to each side of the fish.

8. Repeat Steps 1-7 to make a total of 2 Blue Runner Fish.

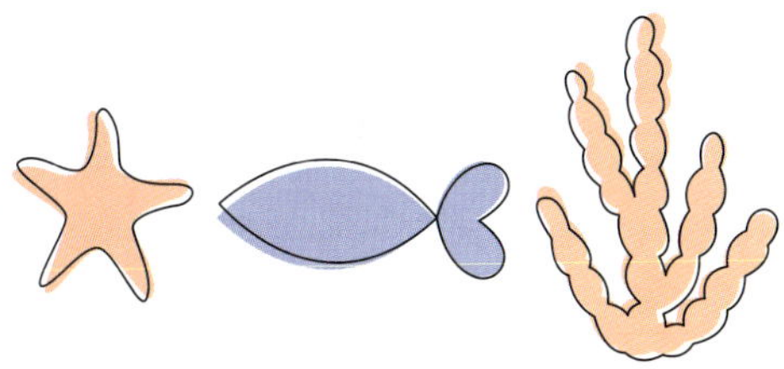

CORAL, SEAWEED, AND STARFISH

Finished Sizes: Coral 4" x 5 1/2", Seaweed 5 1/2" x 7 5/8", Starfish 4" x 4"

SHOPPING LIST

***Note:** Supplies listed are for making 2 coral, 3 seaweed, and 2 starfish.*

- ☐ 1 sheet of orange felt
- ☐ 2 sheets of green felt
- ☐ 1 sheet of yellow felt

*Please read **General Instructions**, pages 30-31, before beginning project. Follow **Using Patterns**, page 30, to adjust pattern size.*

CUTTING

***Note:** Use patterns on page 27.*

1. Cut 2 coral from orange felt.
2. Cut 3 seaweed from green felt.
3. Cut 2 starfish from yellow felt.

SHERBET FISH

Finished Size: 6" x 4 1/2"

SHOPPING LIST

Note: *Supplies listed are for making 1 fish.*

- ☐ 1 sheet of orange felt
- ☐ 1 sheet of yellow felt
- ☐ 1 sheet of white felt
- ☐ 1 sheet of black felt
- ☐ orange 6-strand embroidery floss
- ☐ embroidery needle
- ☐ heavy-duty magnet
- ☐ polyester fiberfill
- ☐ low-temp glue gun and glue sticks

*Please read **General Instructions**, pages 30-31, before beginning project. Follow **Using Patterns**, page 30, to adjust pattern size.*

CUTTING

Note: *Use patterns on page 28.*

1. Cut 2 bodies from orange felt.
2. Cut 1 tail fin from yellow felt.
3. Cut 2 outer eyes from white felt.
4. Cut 2 inner eyes from black felt.

TO MAKE THE SHERBET FISH

Note: *Refer to **Embroidery Stitches**, page 31, for stitch techniques. Use 3 strands of floss for all stitching unless otherwise indicated.*

1. Using a Backstitch, stitch 3 circles on 1 body using 6 strands of embroidery floss. Repeat for the other body.

2. Glue a magnet near the front on one body; be sure to leave enough space to stitch the fish together later.

3. Stack the bodies. Glue the tail fin between the bodies. Be careful not to put glue in the area where you will stitch to assemble the fish. Using a Running Stitch, stitch the bodies together, leaving an opening at the bottom for stuffing using embroidery floss.

4. Stuff fish with fiberfill. Continue the Running Stitch to close the opening.

5. Glue the eyes to each side of the fish.

INKY THE OCTOPUS

Finished Size: 5" x 5 1/2"

SHOPPING LIST

Note: *Supplies listed are for making 1 octopus.*

- ☐ 1 sheet of purple felt
- ☐ 1 sheet of black felt
- ☐ purple 6-strand embroidery floss
- ☐ embroidery needle
- ☐ heavy-duty magnet
- ☐ polyester fiberfill
- ☐ low-temp glue gun and glue sticks

*Please read **General Instructions**, pages 30-31, before beginning project. Follow **Using Patterns**, page 30, to adjust pattern size.*

CUTTING

Note: *Use patterns on page 27.*

1. Cut 2 bodies from purple felt.
2. Cut 4 eyes from black felt.

TO MAKE THE OCTOPUS

Note: *Refer to **Embroidery Stitches**, page 31, for stitch technique. Use 3 strands of floss for all stitching.*

1. Glue a magnet near the top on one body; be sure to leave enough space to stitch the octopus together later.

2. Stack the bodies. Using a Running Stitch, stitch the bodies together, leaving an opening for stuffing and using embroidery floss.

3. Stuff octopus with fiberfill. Continue the Running Stitch to close the opening.

4. Glue the eyes to each side of the octopus.

TACO PLUSHIE

Finished Size: 15" x 10"

SHOPPING LIST

- ☐ 16" x 38" piece of gold felt
- ☐ 16" x 22" piece of brown felt
- ☐ 3 sheets of light green felt
- ☐ 1 sheet of red felt
- ☐ 1 sheet of black felt
- ☐ gold 6-strand embroidery floss
- ☐ embroidery needle
- ☐ polyester fiberfill
- ☐ low-temp glue gun and glue sticks

*Please read **General Instructions**, pages 30-31, before beginning project. Follow **Using Patterns**, page 30.*

CUTTING

***Note:** Use patterns on page 29.*

1. Cut 2 rectangles 15" x 18" from gold felt. Stack the rectangles together. Round the corners to make 2 taco shells. We used a large oval platter as a guide.
2. Cut 2 rectangles 15" x 10" from brown felt. Stack the rectangles together. Scallop the edges to make taco meat.
3. Cut 6 lettuce leaves from light green felt.
4. Cut random pairs of squares and rectangles from red felt for tomatoes.
5. Cut 2 eyes and 1 mouth from black felt.

TO MAKE THE TACO PLUSHIE

***Note:** Refer to **Embroidery Stitches**, page 31, for stitch techniques. Use 3 strands of floss for all stitching unless otherwise indicated.*

1. Using a Running Stitch, stitch the taco shells together using embroidery floss and leaving an opening for stuffing.
2. Stuff the taco shell lightly with fiberfill. Continue the Running Stitch to sew the opening closed.
3. Glue 2 lettuce leaves together, leaving an opening for stuffing. Stuff the lettuce leaf lightly with fiberfill. Glue the opening closed. Repeat to make a total of 3 lettuce leaves.
4. Repeat Step 3 with the taco meat.
5. Fold the taco shell in half and insert taco meat and lettuce leaves. Move the pieces around until they fit as desired; glue pieces together.
6. Glue pairs of tomato pieces together. Glue the tomato pieces as desired in taco.
7. Glue the eyes and mouth to the taco shell.

PATTERNS

Leisure Arts, Inc., grants permission to the owner of this book to photocopy the patterns on pages 22-29 for personal use only.

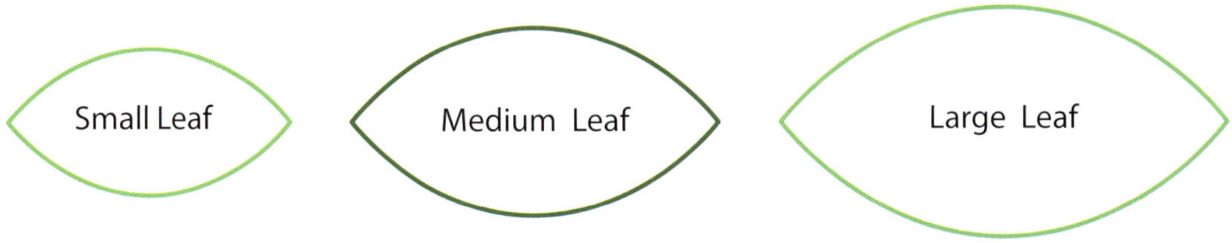

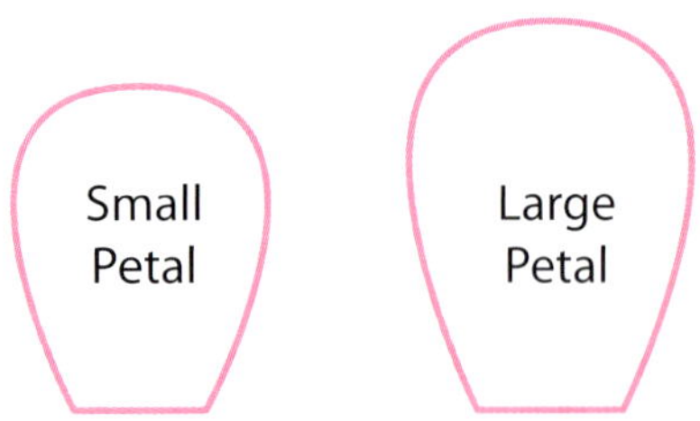

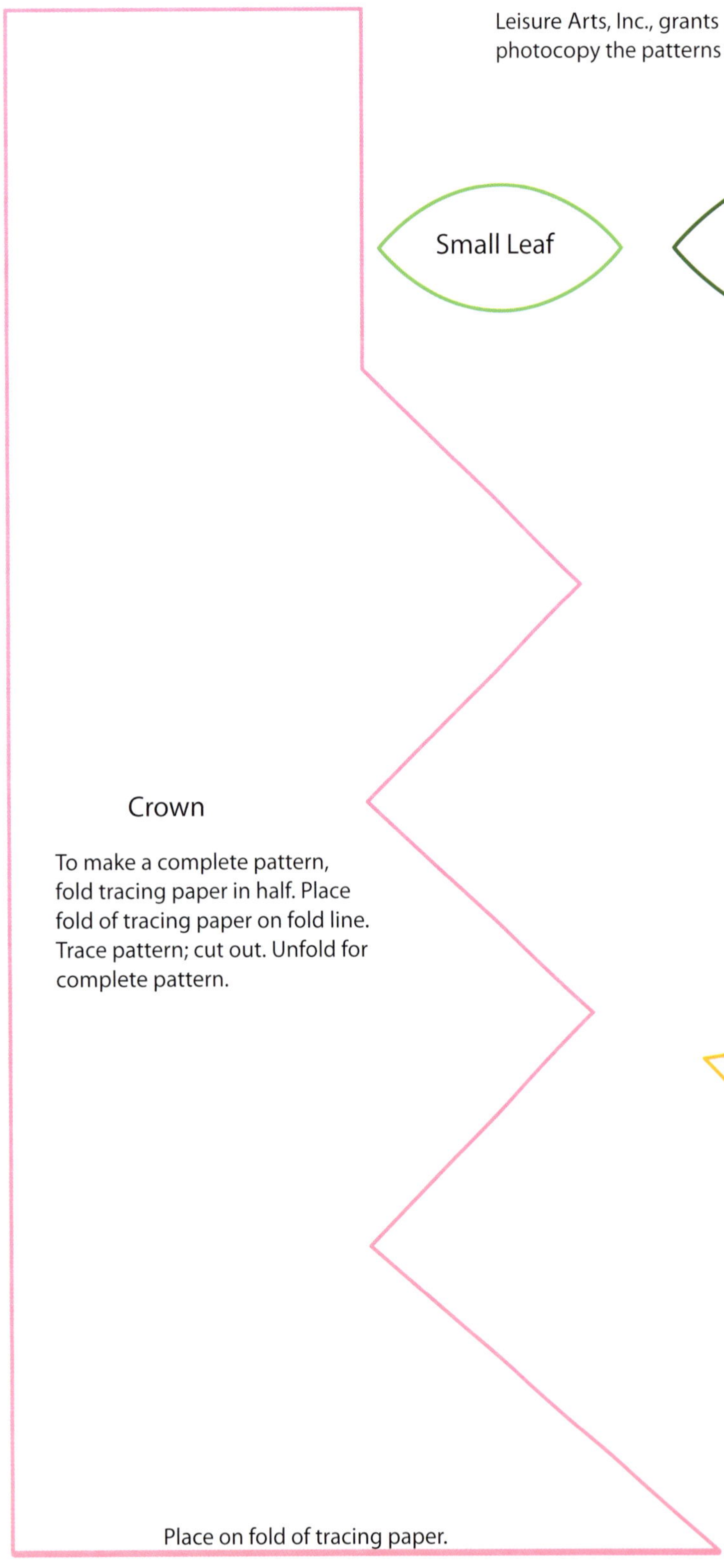

**Enlarge Page to 125%

**Enlarge Page to 125%

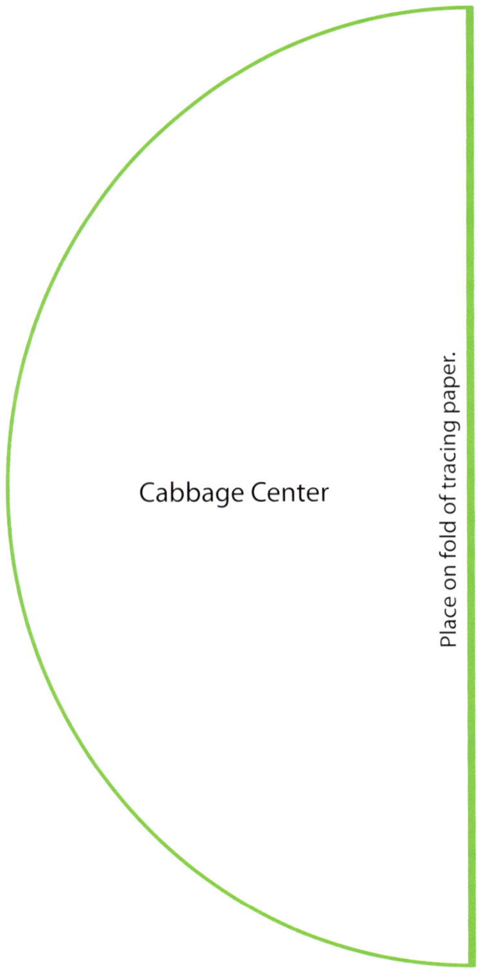

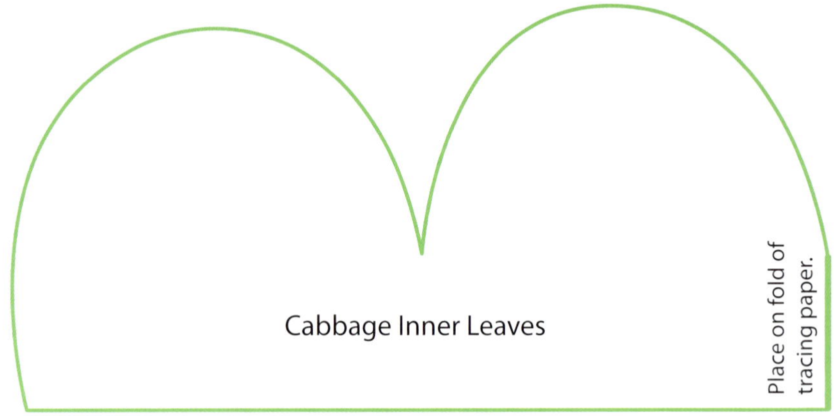

To make a complete pattern, fold tracing paper in half. Place fold of tracing paper on fold line. Trace pattern; cut out. Unfold for complete pattern.

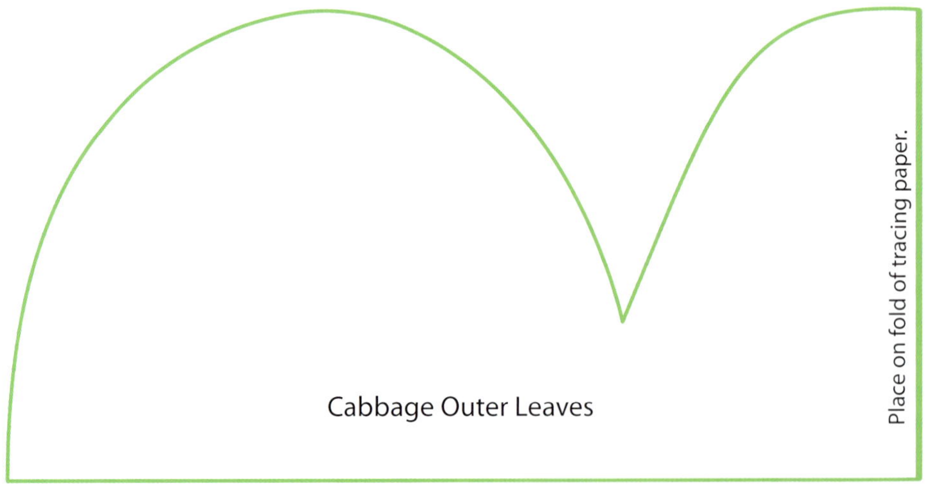

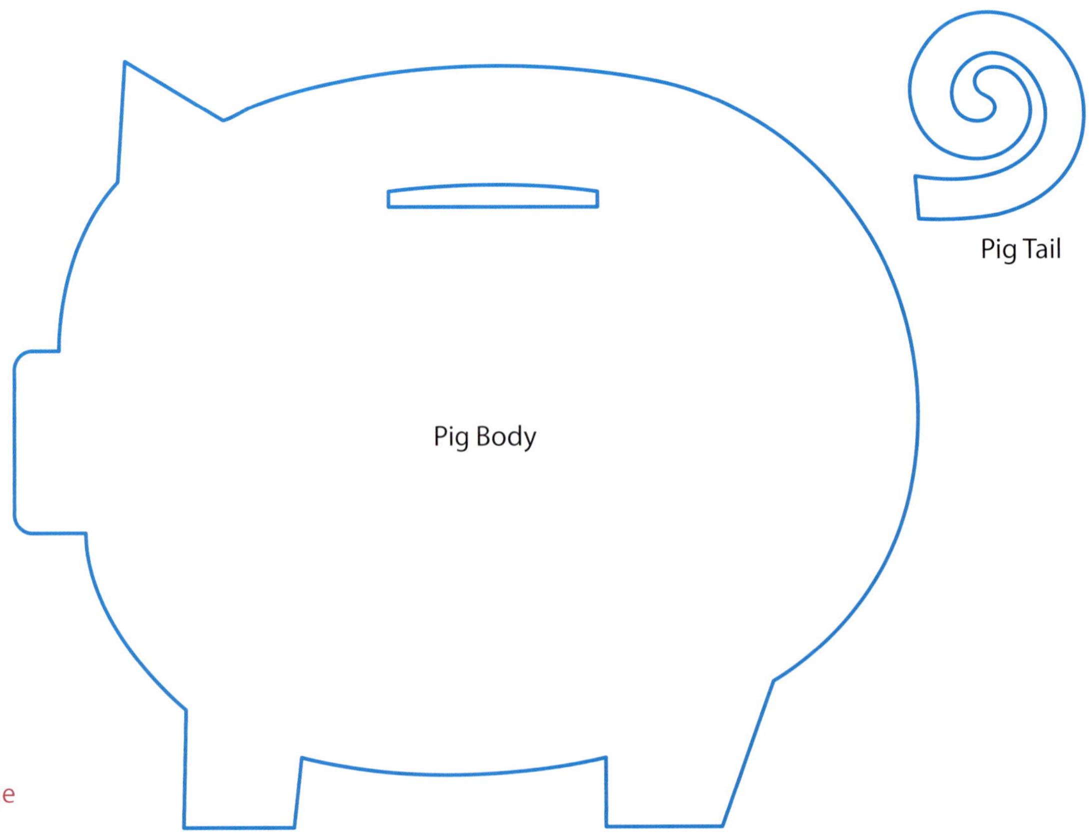

**DO NOT Enlarge Page

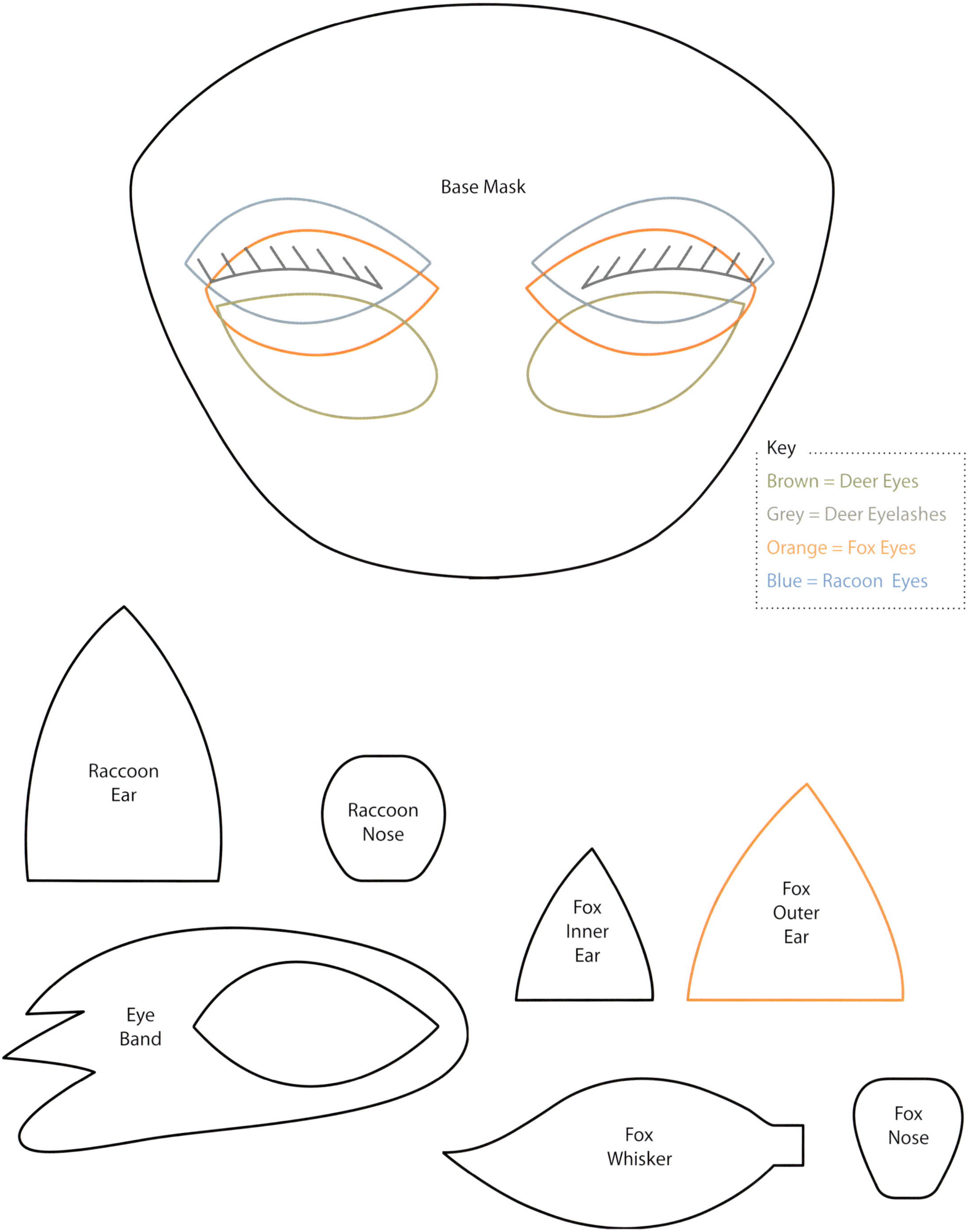

**Enlarge Page to 125%

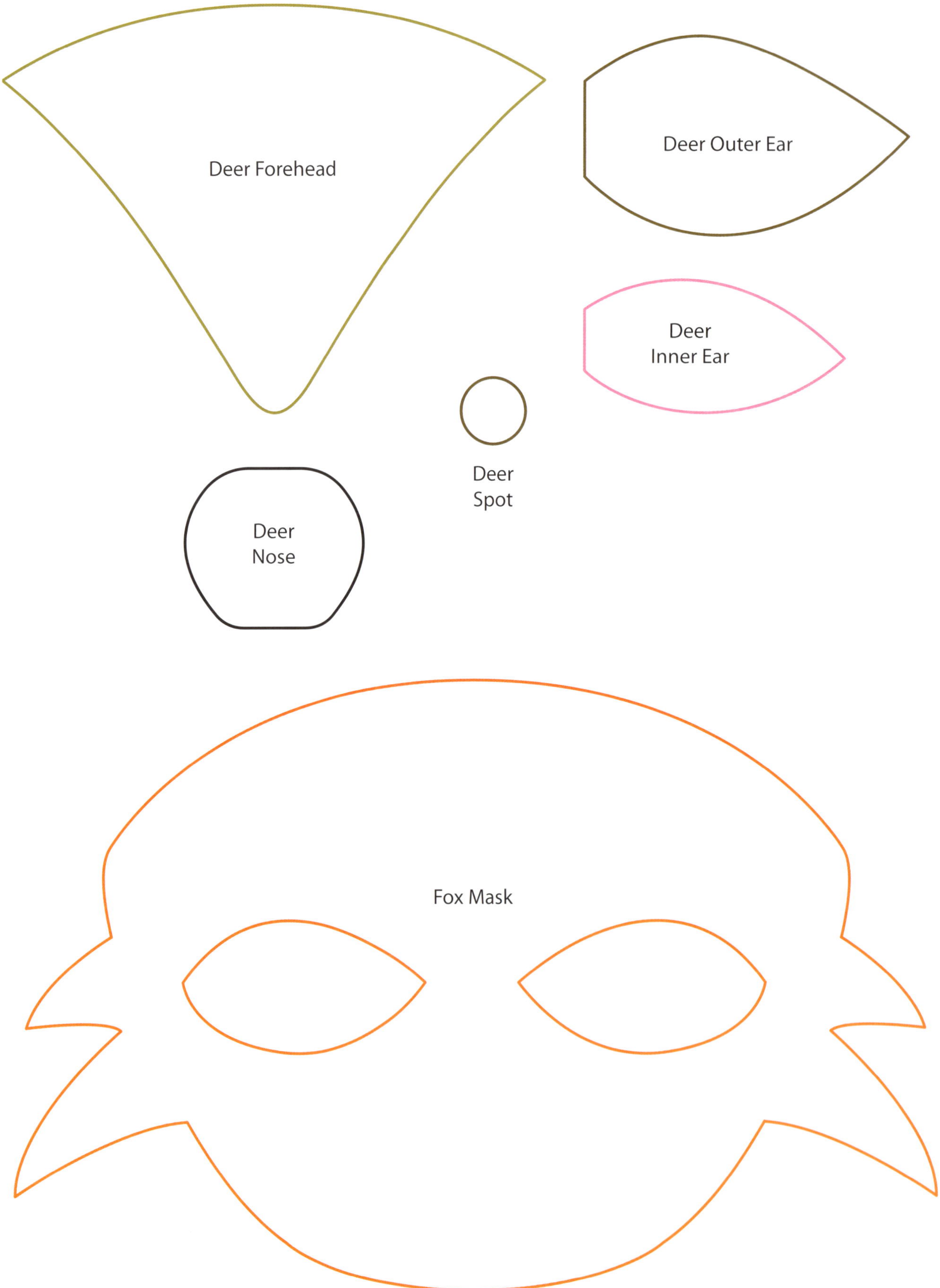

**Enlarge Page to 125%

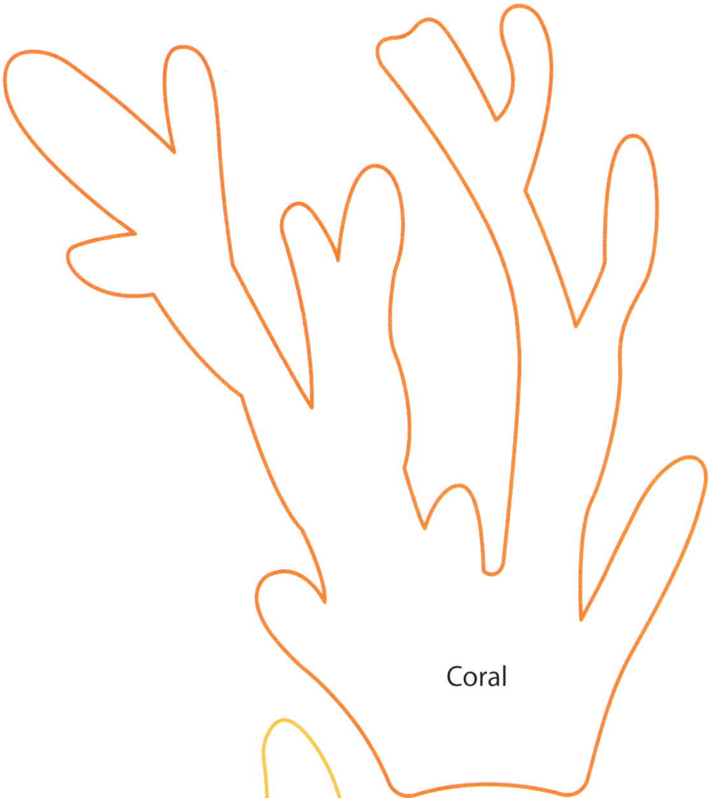

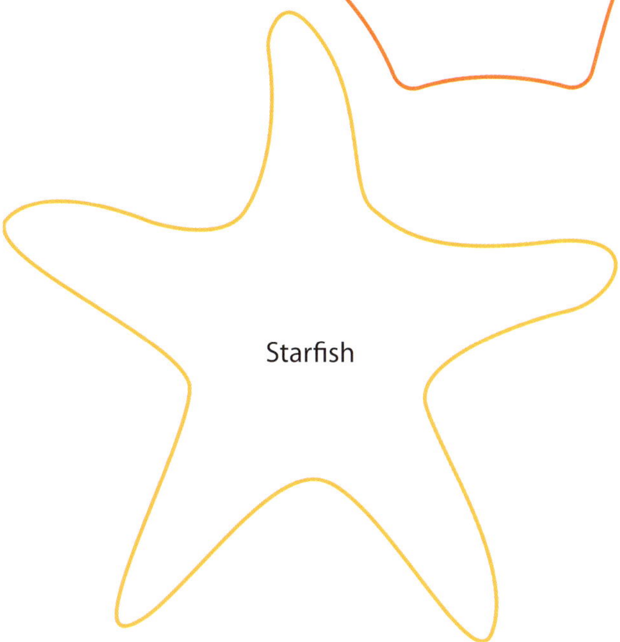

Inky the
Octopus Eye

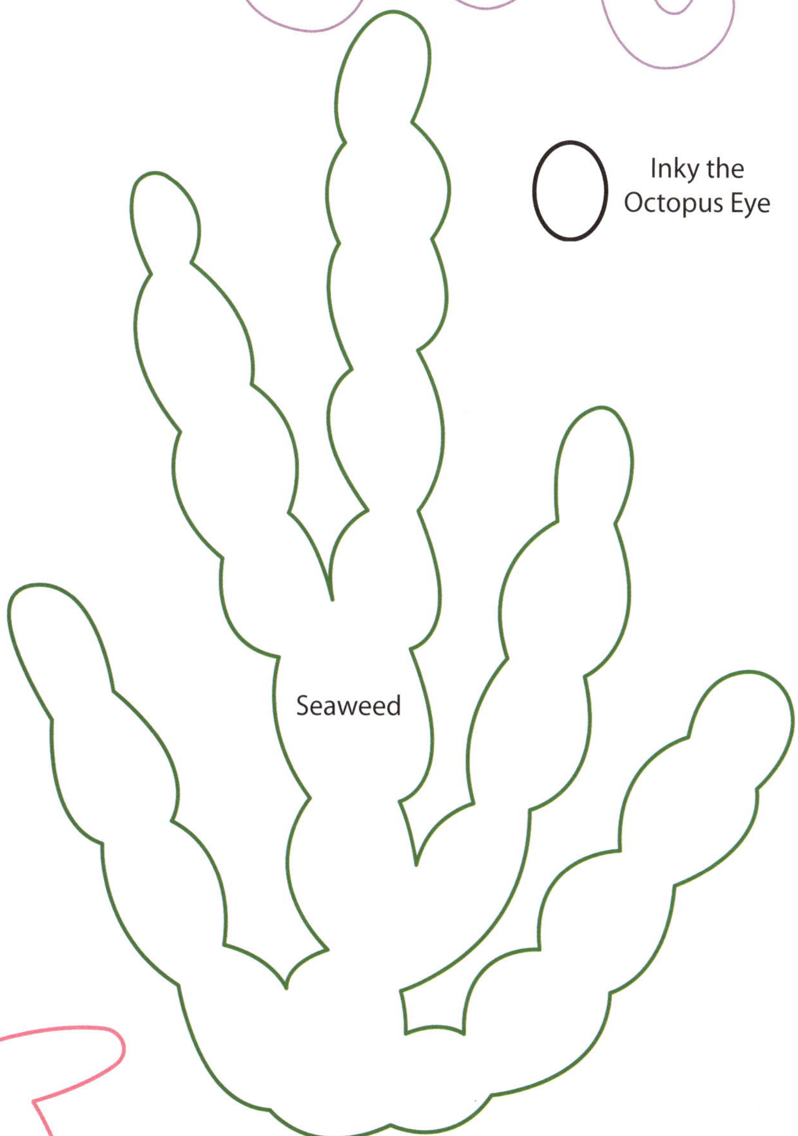

Pinky Fish
Outer Eye

Pinky Fish
Inner Eye

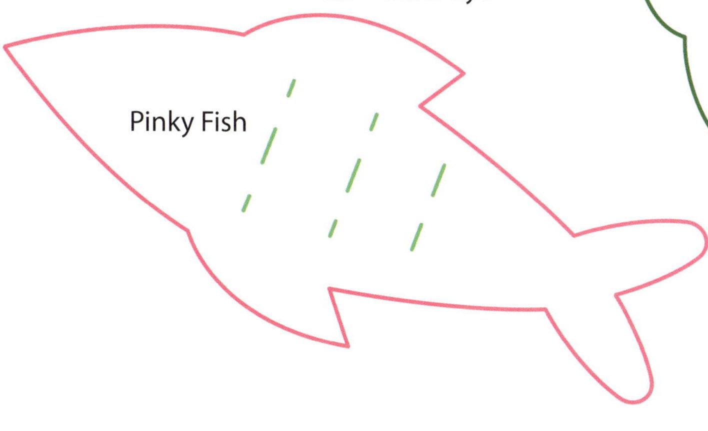

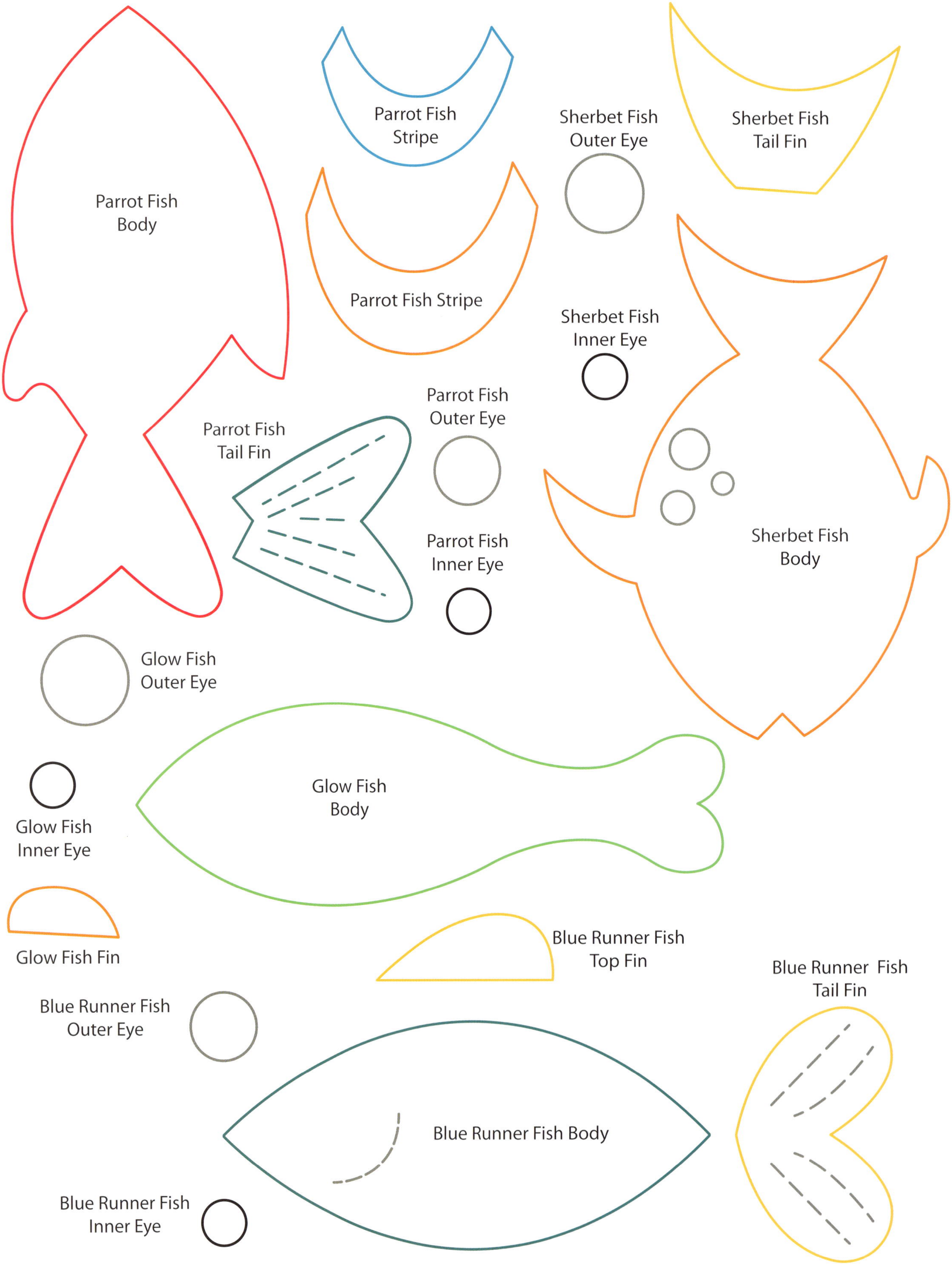

**Enlarge Page to 130%

Taco Face

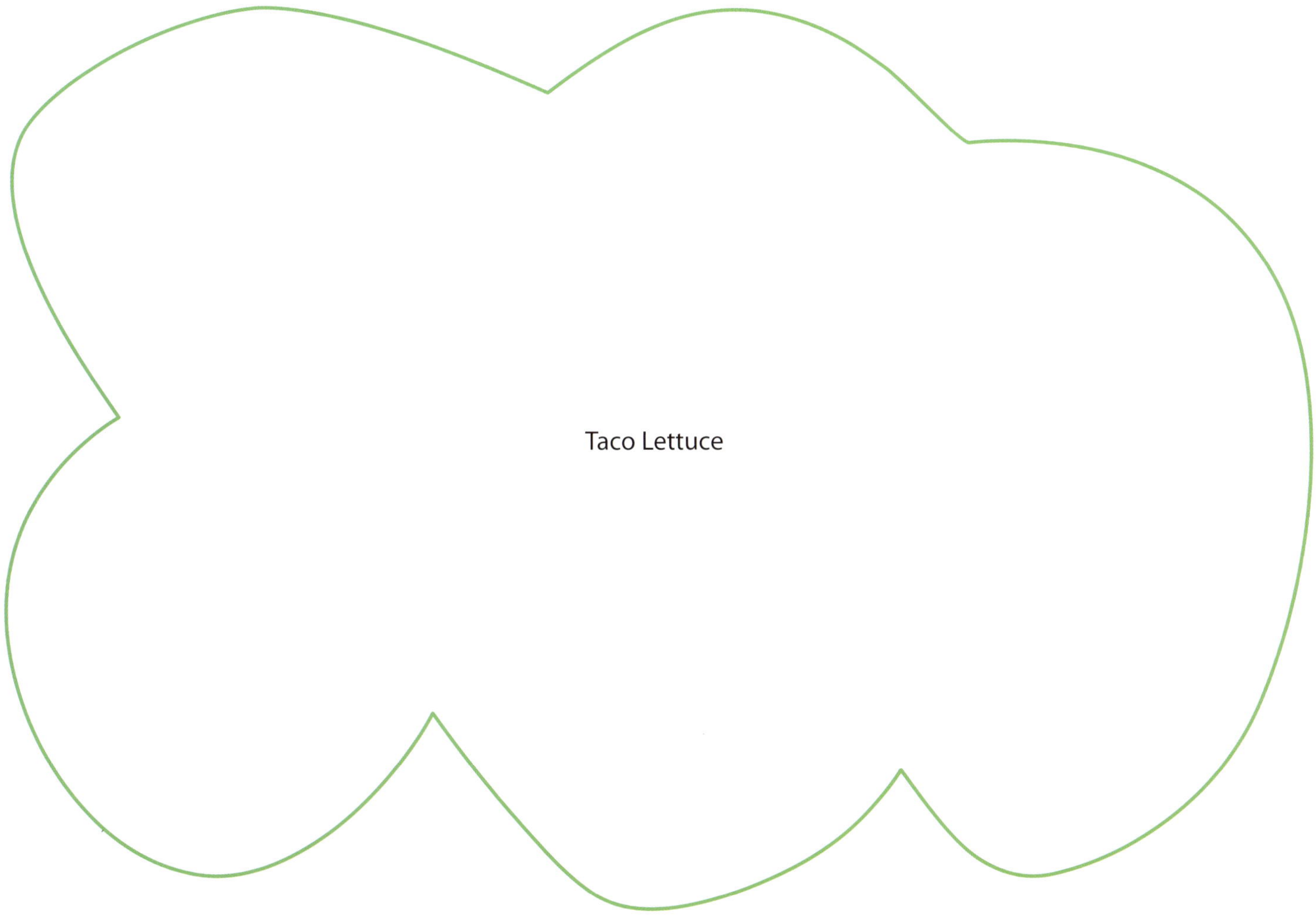

Taco Lettuce

**DO NOT Enlarge Page

GENERAL INSTRUCTIONS

To make your crafting easier and more enjoyable, we encourage you to carefully read all of the General Instructions and familiarize yourself with the individual project instructions before you get started.

SUPPLIES

Supplies listed below are needed for all projects. Individual project instructions include supplies specific to that project.

FELT

Projects were made using wool felt or eco-felt. Eco-felt is made using Eco-fil™, a polyester fiber created from 100% post-consumer recycled plastic bottles. Both wool felt and eco-felt are available in approximately 9" x 12" sheets or by the yard in 36", 60", or 72" widths. Press felt using a pressing cloth.

THREAD

Projects were stitched using six-strand cotton embroidery floss. Individual project instructions specify the number of strands to use.

NEEDLES

A sharp point is necessary to pierce felt, but the size and type of needle is an individual choice. The eye needs to be large enough to accommodate the number of strands of floss you will be using.

Embroidery needles, sometimes referred to as crewel needles, usually work well. Sizes range from #3 - #10 and they are available in individual and multi-size packages. Keep in mind that the lower the number, the larger the needle.

SCISSORS

Use fabric scissors to cut out felt shapes and utility scissors for cutting paper patterns. Small sharp embroidery scissors are handy for clipping thread and trimming "fuzzies" from the edges of finished shapes.

USING PATTERNS

Some patterns in this book may need to be enlarged. The percentage to enlarge the pattern is stated at the bottom of the pattern page. Photocopy the patterns, enlarging as directed. Cut out pattern on outer line.

WORKING WITH FELT

Place patterns, printed side up, on felt; pin. Cut out shapes even with edges of pattern. Repeat for each pattern piece needed for your project.

Felt does not have a right or wrong side. If a felt shape is embroidered, the stitched side becomes the right side. When instructed to layer shapes, place an embroidered shape right side up on top of another shape. For shapes that are not embroidered, simply layer the shapes.

EMBROIDERY STITCHES

BACKSTITCH

Come up at 1, go down, at 2, and come up at 3 (**Fig. 1**). Length of stitches may be varied as desired.

Fig. 1

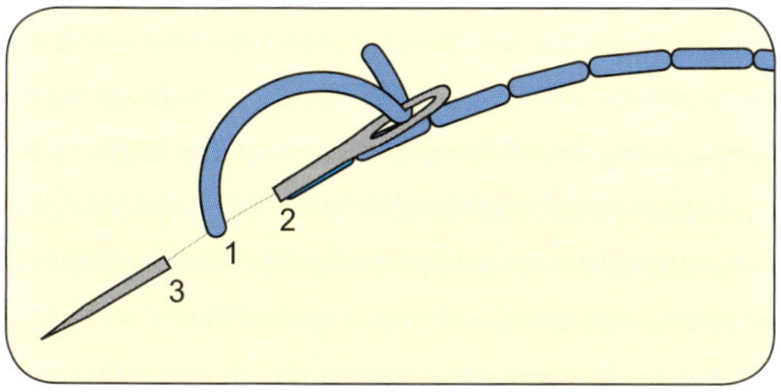

STRAIGHT STITCH

Come up at 1 and go down at 2 (**Fig. 3**). Length of stitches may be varied as desired.

Fig. 3

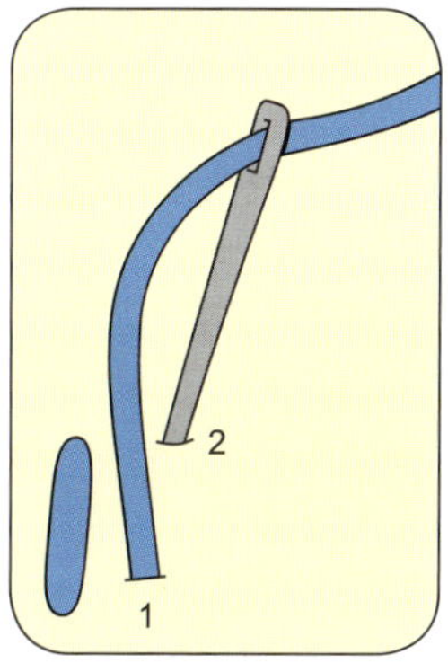

RUNNING STITCH

The running stitch consists of a series of straight stitches with the stitch length equal to the space between stitches. Come up at 1 and go down at 2. Come up at 3 and go down at 4 (**Fig. 2**).

Fig. 2

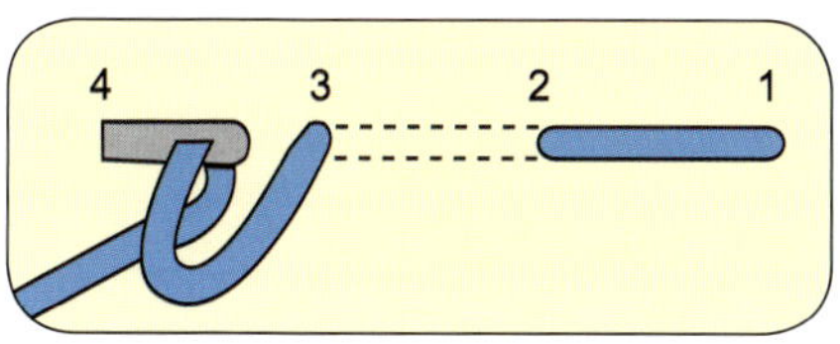

WHIPSTITCH

Matching raw edges, place shapes together. Come up at 1 and go down at 2 (**Fig. 4**) so that the thread overcasts the edges of the shape.

Fig. 4

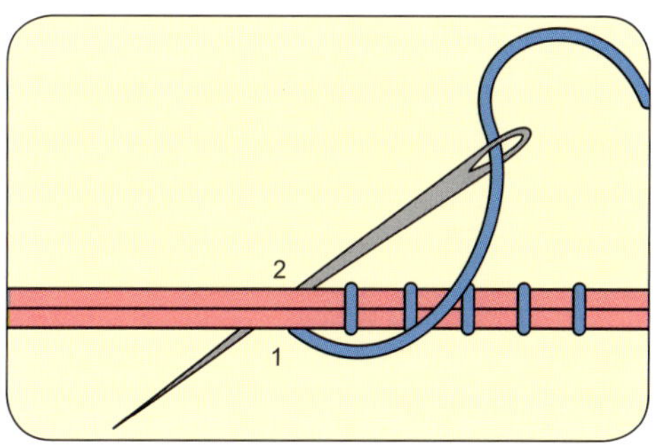

meet KIM LAYTON

Driven by a lifelong love of making things, Kimberly Layton took her crafting to a whole new level in 2008. She is now a full-time professional blogger, craft book author, and creative business coach.

Kimberly blogs about Etsy business and all manner of DIY crafty things at EverythingEtsy.com, shares tutorials and inspiring creative ideas at HandmadeandCraft.com, and reveals a more personal side at KimberlyLayton.com. She also can be found as @EverythingEtsy on Twitter, Facebook, Instagram, and Pinterest.

"I like dabbling in all kinds of crafts, but felt is my favorite," she says. Her blogging "all started with trying to promote my felt crafts that I sold in my Etsy shop. From there it grew to coaching and social media training for handmade businesses."

Traveling is Kim's other favorite pastime. "We've visited all the states in the lower 48 and have traveled with our children as far away as the Great Barrier Reef! Just mention the word 'go' and we are there!"

Copyright © 2017 by Leisure Arts, Inc., 104 Champs Blvd., STE 100, Maumelle, AR 72113-6738, www.leisurearts.com. All rights reserved. This publication is protected under federal copyright laws. Reproduction or distribution of this publication or any other Leisure Arts publication, including publications which are out of print, is prohibited unless specifically authorized. This includes, but is not limited to, any form of reproduction or distribution on or through the Internet, including posting, scanning, or e-mail transmission.

We have made every effort to ensure that these instructions are accurate and complete. We cannot, however, be responsible for human error, typographical mistakes, or variations in individual work.

Production Team: Technical Writer – Lisa Lancaster; Technical Associate – Mary Sullivan Hutcheson; Editorial Writer – Susan Frantz Wiles; Senior Graphic Artist – Lora Puls; Graphic Artist – Kytanna McFarlin; Contributing Graphic Artists – Austin Beck and Julian Lyden; Photostylist – Lori Wenger; Photographer – Jason Masters.